THE LIFE & TIMES OF
POL POT

THE LIFE & TIMES OF

Pol Pot

BY
Sandy Noble

This edition first published by
Parragon Book Service Ltd in 1996

Parragon Book Service Ltd
Unit 13–17 Avonbridge Trading Estate
Atlantic Road, Avonmouth
Bristol BS11 9QD

Produced by Magpie Books,
an imprint of Robinson Publishing

ISBN 0 75251 777 5

A copy of the British Library Cataloguing in Publication
Data is available from the British Library.

Typeset by Whitelaw & Palmer Ltd, Glasgow
Printed in Singapore

In most of the world, the name 'Pol Pot' is synonymous with genocide. Films such as *The Killing Fields* reflect the horror that outsiders feel when the recent history of Cambodia is mentioned. Pol Pot stands between the monsters of twentieth-century history, Hitler and Stalin, as the cause, whether deliberate or not, of huge numbers of deaths. His tally may not have been as high as those of his rivals in gross numbers, but it represents a high percentage of the population; there were 8 million Cambodians before he came to power, and about 1 *million fewer* by the time he was ousted. Unlike his mentors, though, Pol Pot has always been very elusive, keeping a low profile, avoiding the cult of personality that has been a feature of virtually all twentieth-century totalitarian dictators, whether Fascist or Nazi, like Franco, Mussolini and Hitler, or Communist like Stalin and Mao Tse-tung. Pol Pot's shadowiness has made him seem more menacing than his rivals; furthermore he is still alive, waiting in the jungle on the Thai border or in northern Cambodia with the fearsome Khmer Rouge (Red, i.e. Communist Khmer) for an opportunity to make a comeback.

Sculpture at Angkor Wat

YOUTH AND EDUCATION

Cambodia has always been in a geopolitical backwater. Its last period of power was in the early Middle Ages under the Khmer kings. Cambodian independence, thereafter, was under constant threat from frequent Thai and Vietnamese invasions. In 1863 the French arrived and tied Cambodia into the economy of Vietnam, of which they were the colonial masters. Cambodians, including royalty, chafed at French rule, but apart from a rebellion in the 1880s did nothing to try to expel them. The royal household, though, formed an island, cut off from the world and its events, and much of its activity was ceremonial – supervising Cambodian Buddhism and putting on the royal ballet (Cambodian ballet was a religious ritual, acting out stories from Buddhist and Hindu myth).

Pol Pot was born Saloth Sar in Prek Sbauv, a village 140 kilometres north of Phnom Penh. His parents were prosperous peasants, and Pol Pot was the eighth of their nine children. His birth date is uncertain: French records give it as 25 May 1928, while North Korean Radio (never the most accurate source of information) in a 1977 broadcast gave it as 1925. When he was six or seven years old he was sent to the royal household at Phnom Penh, it being customary in Cambodia for parents of large families to farm their children out with

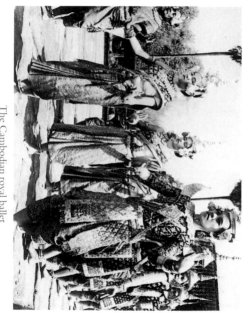

The Cambodian royal ballet

relatives. His cousin Meak had preceded him there, becoming first a dancer and then the chief mistress of Prince Monivong, who had become king in 1927. One of Pol Pot's elder brothers, Loth Suong, had also gone there to become a clerk in the royal palace, and Pol Pot moved in with his cousin and brother. He attended a Buddhist monastery at Vat Botum Vaddei, and there he imbibed Buddhist precepts and discipline. His early years, then, were spent in hermetic seclusion, learning much effectively by rote, where the rules and rituals of a creed, whether religious or political, were considered final, just as the movements of the ritual ballets were so minutely formalized as to allow no individual freedom of expression.

Towards the end of the 1930s, Cambodia began to show the first signs of creating a renewed national identity, while in Vietnam the newly formed Communist Party engaged in physical rebellion against the French authorities. Three Cambodians, Son Ngoc Thanh, Sim Var and Pach Chhoeun, with permission from the French, founded the first Khmer-language newspaper, whose editorial aim was to encourage Cambodians to compete against the Chinese and Vietnamese merchants who dominated the economy. Education became something more of a priority in Cambodia, where there was only a small educated elite (partly because the royal family regarded an educated population as ungovernable). Those who were lucky enough to go on to secondary education, either at French schools in Cambodia or in Saigon, were so few in the 1930s that a very high proportion of them ended up in senior government positions in later years.

Part of the royal palace, Phnom Penh

Pol Pot went to the École Miche, a Catholic primary school when he was eight, and stayed there for six years. There he mixed with French and Vietnamese children and acquired the rudiments of a Western education, and learnt French. Towards the end of this period the Thais took advantage of the fall of France in June 1940 and the Japanese threat from China (which Japan had invaded in 1937), against France's South-East Asian colonies, to invade Cambodia in 1940–41, and annexed the provinces of Battambang and Siem Reap in the north-west. This catastrophe led to the decline and death of King Monivong. The French appointed his grandson Norodom Sihanouk as the new king.

The French then cast around for ways to improve the prestige of the monarchy and decided to found a secondary school in

Kompong Cham, The Collège Norodom Sihanouk to which Pol Pot was sent. At about the time of his enrolment, there was, by Cambodian standards, a major political event; Son Ngoc Thanh and Pach Chhoeun organized a 500-strong demonstration against the French, after the latter had arrested two Buddhist monks for disseminating anti-French propaganda among the local militia. Chhoeun was arrested and thrown into jail, while Thanh went into hiding, going via Battambang to Japan where he spent most of the rest of the war.

The Second World War came closer to Cambodia in 1944, when France was liberated, and, under General de Gaulle, decided to reassert its control over its colonies, also agreeing to help the Allies in the continuing war against Japan. In Vietnam, the Viet Minh (the resistance organization led by Ho Chi Minh) attacked Japanese positions and the Americans bombed both Phnom Penh and the coastal waters of Indochina. The Japanese response, in March 1945, was to take over Cambodia, intern French officials, including the school-teachers at Sihanouk College, throughout Indochina, and to persuade the Vietnamese, Laotians and Cambodians to declare independence from France, which Sihanouk did on 11 March 1945. Son Ngoc Thanh returned from Japan to become first Foreign Minister, and then Prime Minister in May. He did his best to keep Cambodia independent, but in September, after Japan had surrendered, the French returned, freeing their officials, and persuading Sihanouk to restore the *status quo ante*, albeit with the establishment of political parties and a written constitution. Thanh was arrested and exiled to France.

In 1947 Pol Pot became a carpentry student at the Russey Keo École Technique (technical college). In later years, Pol Pot was to use this period of technical education to show that he was a 'man of the people', just as he would describe his childhood as having taken place on a peasant smallholding. At this time too, he met Ieng Sary, who would later be instrumental in guiding the communist revolution in Cambodia.

New political parties, whose existence the French had approved, began to be active: elections were held and proved an overwhelming victory (fifty out of sixty-seven seats on a committee to approve a constitution) for the Democratic Party, led by Prince Sisowath Yuthevong. Yuthevong had spent much of his life in French academia, and had a relatively modern constitutional outlook, and because of his absence he was not tainted by palace intrigue. In the elections to the National Assembly, the Democrats won fifty out of seventy-five seats, despite French support for conservative elements. Pol Pot and Ieng Sary both worked for the Democrats.

In 1949 – the year in which France granted Cambodia partial independence – Pol Pot went to study in Paris on a government scholarship as one of a contingent of 100 Cambodians. It is not clear why he was chosen for a scholarship, but it may have been a reward for working for the Democrats. They also wanted to build an educated Cambodian technical class to challenge the Chinese and Vietnamese stranglehold on commerce.

For his summer holiday in 1950, Pol Pot

went to work in Yugoslavia. Because Yugoslavia was in such a parlous position – cut off from the capitalist West, cut off from the Soviet Union – mobilization of the population for the building of public works was instituted on a widespread scale, just as it had been in the Soviet Union in the 1920s. Pol Pot was highly impressed by this mobilization, and by the organized productivity of the population, and would use it as a model when he came into power.

Ieng Sary arrived in Paris in 1950 and the two men joined the French Communist Party. At the time, communism seemed nothing but a huge success story. Stalin was still in power in Russia, while Mao Tse-tung had defeated the Nationalists in China; in France the Communist Party was extremely powerful. Communism seemed to be here to stay, and also the

Phnom Penh in settled times

logical choice for any forward-looking intellectual. Before coming to Paris Ieng Sary, with
another activist, Rath Samoeun, had led a student strike at the Lycée Sisowath against the
French school authorities. Their reward from
the Cambodian Government had been scholarships to further their education in France.
Once arrived they threw their efforts into
organizing indoctrination meetings, where fel-
low Cambodians could discuss Marxist-
Leninism (many Cambodians seemed to think
Marx and Lenin were one person – Max-
Lenin!).

The sort of communism then prevalent in
France was Stalinist. It is thought, too, that
Pol Pot read Stalin's *History of the Communist
Party of the Soviet Union*. Stalin's view of the
world was that of a continuous conspiracy of
anti-communist forces, both within and

without the Soviet Union, against which one had always to be vigilant and ruthless. Stalin had conducted show trials in the 1930s against many senior members of the Party whom he had viewed as possible rivals – initially because they did not automatically agree with every view he put forward, later because he thought they might not agree. Given the closed nature of Soviet society, its limited contacts with the outside world, it is hard to see how anti-communist influence could have crept in. Pol Pot was to absorb Stalin's view of the world, based on the same irrational fears.

While Pol Pot was in Paris, King Sihanouk had become increasingly disenchanted with the Democratic Party. Its leader, Ieu Koeuss, was assassinated in January 1950 and it was suspected that the king or the French had had a hand in this, or that it was the responsibility of Yem Sambaur, the Prime Minister who took over after Sihanouk had dissolved the Democrat-dominated National Assembly. Sihanouk was gradually edging his country back to monarchical autocracy. But if this was a move in one direction, there was, meanwhile, a move in another.

The Indochina Communist Party, entirely dominated by the Vietnamese, decided in February 1950 that it should encourage liberation struggles in Laos and Cambodia – liberation from colonialism and from the existing backward socio-political system. The Party had been recruiting in Cambodia for over a year, and thought that with Vietnamese leadership and some indoctrination, the peasants could be roused to liberate themselves. The Indochina Communist Party was then divided into three parts, representing Cambodia, Laos and Vietnam, with the last being the senior partner. The Cambodian People's Revolutionary Party was led by Son Ngoc Minh, who had been a communist since the middle of the Second World War.

Back in Cambodia new elections were to be held in 1951. The Cambodian students in Paris mostly hoped that Son Ngoc Thanh could return to lead the Democratic Party. Sihanouk asked the French to allow him to return and they eventually agreed, after the elections had been held. Thanh's return was a major event, met by great public acclaim. Shortly afterwards the French High Commissioner was assassinated in Phnom Penh. The feeling in Paris was that an anti-colonial revolution was beginning to stir, and this view was reinforced by Thanh's refusal to join

King Sihanouk after his return to Cambodia

the Government – instead, he disappeared into the Cambodian hinterland to link up with anti-French guerrillas near Siem Reap. He was joined there by several students from the Lycée Sisowath. Discussions were held between his group and the Vietnamese-led communist guerrillas, but nothing came of them, and essentially Thanh faded from the picture. His espousal of military action in the anti-colonial cause had alarmed Sihanouk and the French. Sihanouk had only agreed to seek Thanh's return because of the weight of popular pressure, and had expected him to become part of legitimate government, not a focus of violent opposition. Sihanouk requested extra troops from the French, which were sent. In June 1952 he dissolved the National Assembly and began to rule by decree, effectively re-establishing an absolute monarchy. In Paris, Pol Pot denounced this development in the Cambodian student magazine, declaring that absolute monarchy was 'a running sore'. He also pointed out revolutionary parallels – France and Russia – where the monarchy had disappeared; it was simply a burden on the people, impoverishing and oppressing them.

The Cambodian government reacted by withdrawing the scholarships of the politically active students, though it is not clear whether they did so for Pol Pot – as he had failed to sit any examinations, he had gained no qualifications, and may well have had his scholarship withdrawn for being academically inadequate. After losing it, Pol Pot remained in Paris for another five months, and it was probably during this period that he joined the Communist Party. An academic career was closed to him, either in France or Cambodia, but the Party offered an alternative future. It was also a party in which a self-effacing character such as Pol Pot could progress through sheer dedication, loyalty and organizational skills.

RETURN TO CAMBODIA

Pol Pot was back in Cambodia in 1953. Initially he stayed with his brother, Loth Suong, in Phnom Penh, but within a month he had joined the communist resistance. Because the Cambodian Communist Party wanted to keep its activities secret, Pol Pot pretended that he was working with the non-communist resistance, though sources state that this was not true. He joined the Indochina Communist Party (ICP), dominated by the Viet Minh. Accounts differ as to his role – some sources state that the Cambodians were given menial tasks by the Vietnamese – but there is no doubt that he was held in some esteem as he was not assigned to a combat group but to a propaganda section in the communists' headquarters; he also attended cadre school (using cadres or cells of a few highly politicized members was the preferred method of communist infiltration of society). Pol Pot's connections with several different strata of Cambodian society, and the time he had spent in France, which in theory gave him a more sophisticated outlook, were of value to the Vietnamese. His mentor in the ICP was Tou Samouth, who had joined the ICP in 1946 and worked among the Khmer minority in Vietnam and in eastern Cambodia, converting peasants to the cause. Tou Samouth came from the Buddhist tradition and was an impassioned teacher, popular with his students. Pol Pot absorbed as much as he could from Tou Samouth, both in style and content; he learnt well and came in turn to be highly regarded as a teacher.

Meanwhile the flames of war were dying down: in November 1953, the French, in response to Sihanouk's urging, granted Cambodia full independence, and also agreed to grant the same to the non-communist nationalists in southern Vietnam (though they continued to fight the communist Viet Minh in northern Vietnam, a war that had begun in 1946). Many of the Cambodian guerrillas laid down their arms and joined Sihanouk's Government. The First Indochina War came to an end in July 1954, shortly after the Viet Minh victory over the French army at Dien Bien Phu. Vietnam was divided at the 17th

Parallel. Guerrillas from other countries – Laos and Cambodia – were given the option of returning home or moving to North Vietnam. Over 1000 Cambodians, including many of Pol Pot's friends and those who would be later members of his Government, chose the latter option. Pol Pot returned to Phnom Penh as an activist for the ICP.

The Geneva agreement of 1954 had stipulated that a new National Assembly should be elected in Cambodia, and once again the Democratic Party began to stir into action. Sihanouk had different ideas: he had enjoyed his period of absolute control and thought that he should have most of the credit for achieving Cambodian independence. Within the Democratic Party, there was a change of leadership, as Thiounn Mumm and others of Pol Pot's colleagues from Paris days took over; they wanted to ensure that Cambodia, having thrown off the French yoke, did not become a US satellite. They were against joining the US's creation, the South-East Asia Treaty Organization (SEATO), a loose anti-communist alliance. Pol Pot worked with the left-moving Democrats and with the Pracheachon Group, another left-wing party that intended to fight in the elections. The Pracheachon Group comprised of former combat guerrillas, uneducated ex-workers and peasants, who took the ICP as their guide. The ICP's plan was that winning the elections was a prelude to further radicalizing the Democratic Party, bringing communism to Cambodia through the back door.

But Prince Sihanouk was equally determined to win the elections. As Prime Minister, he named his father, rather than himself, king, as the constitution did not allow monarchical government, and founded the Sangkum Reastr Niyum (People's Socialist Community). Government workers were forced to join this party or lose their jobs. He gained the support of the Chinese, and declared that Cambodia would take a non-aligned position in the Cold War, thus stealing the foreign policy clothes of the Democrats and the Pracheachon. Sihanouk was virulently anti-communist, declaring that communism would ruin the lives of ordinary Cambodians – in the event an accurate prediction.

The Democrats campaigned vigorously and to dampen their appeal, Sihanouk had Keng Vannsak (one of Pol Pot's mentors in Paris), their leader, arrested. Thiounn Mumm, thinking he would be next, fled to France, and Sihanouk's agents attacked Democratic rallies and campaign workers, several of whom were killed. (Pol Pot was not a target, which suggests that he must have kept a very low profile). This aggression had the required result and led to the Sangkum gaining all ninety-one seats in the National Assembly. Sihanouk held absolute power. He was to hold it for fifteen years.

After the elections, Pol Pot took up a post at a new private college in Phnom Penh, teaching a variety of subjects. Teachers have high status in Cambodia, partly because of the Hindu and Buddhist traditions, and also because of the influence of France, where teachers are still held in high regard. Cambodian teachers adopt a mentorial role, and are expected to impart a wider understanding of life. Pol Pot also held political sessions at home for young people, and is described as having led these meetings without revealing his own views,

Pol Pot

apart from anger at government corruption. It seems to have been known that he was a communist, but this was regarded more as a sign of intellectual and moral rigour, rather than a threat, and it is reported that, in his teaching, Pol Pot followed school policy rather than inserting communist interpretations of history.

Pol Pot operated under several identities – Saloth Sar to his older acquaintances – and Pol to members of the Pracheachon. He was working to build up an organization in Cambodia for the ICP, so that Cambodian communists would be prepared when the moment arrived for them to take a more active role in the political struggle. This was a very cloak-and-dagger period of his life, though Pol Pot was never identified as a subversive or persecuted by the police, unlike other members of the Communist Party. It was during the mid-1950s that he began to work with Nuon Chea, who would become a senior member of the Cambodian Communist Party.

One problem the Party had in Cambodia was that there was no proletariat to speak of – no masses of industrial labourers who could be converted to the cause, which made it a little difficult to adopt the usual Marxist-Leninist approach of inspiring the workers to lead the revolution. This meant that the Party itself had to do so, which it did by recruiting the educated class, a task for which Pol Pot was ideally suited. He did much until he disappeared from Phnom Penh to recruit additional members to the Party, finding fertile ground among students and monks, who were generally more socially aware –

that is, aware of the gross differences in wealth in Cambodian society. This work was supported by other teachers, many of whom were communist and who had shared the intellectual excitement of Paris.

The communists in Cambodia were also careful not to show their true colours – Pol Pot, for example, taught that Sihanouk was the father of independence, and other communists actually worked for Sihanouk. The existence of the Party itself was kept secret. Working with other groups was considered expedient – they could help destroy some of the opposition and then be abandoned themselves when the moment was ripe. Support in the country from ex-resistance fighters was limited – many had disarmed after the Geneva agreement – as they felt that they were inadequately equipped to take on Sihanouk's forces, and any resistance was usually rooted out by the regime. It was also not clear to them what they would gain by overthrowing Sihanouk. Symptomatic of their uncertainty was the defection of their Vietnamese-controlled communist leader, Sieu Heng. This decline in rural support led to the Party's committee in Phnom Penh becoming the chief communist organization for the whole country.

In the late 1950s, South Vietnamese communists began to renew the armed struggle against the pro-Western government in Saigon, the capital of South Vietnam. North Vietnam therefore sought to help them by reactivating the Communist Parties of Cambodia and Laos, (Laos also had a pro-Western government and received considerable US aid). The situation in Cambodia was complicated by the fact that because of his anti-Western stance, Sihanouk was favoured by both Peking and Hanoi (the capital of North Vietnam); thus, though he was anti-communist within Cambodia, his foreign policy could be said to be pro-communist. So while communists in Cambodia could offer him their support, if they did so too openly as communists, they exposed themselves to persecution. Chinese and North Vietnamese support for Sihanouk was to be maintained right into the 1990s, which put local communists in an invidious position; it was Pol Pot who had to deal with this problem when, later, he became leader of the Party.

In September 1960 a congress was held in Hanoi, at which it was resolved to oust the Americans, large numbers of whose military advisers were in South Vietnam, and in the process convert the south to communism. Subsequently, the Cambodian communists held a small congress (twenty-one participants) in one of the buildings at Phnom Penh railway station. This congress was described by Pol Pot's henchmen as the first Cambodian Communist Congress, though there had been an earlier one in 1951. That, however, did not fit in with the communists' self-glamorizing presentation that the Party had enjoyed a seamless ride to power once it had decided to organize and act, and that the same sets of guiding hands were still at the helm. In fact, at this stage North Vietnam provided most of the guidance, having had, of course, considerably more experience of revolutionary struggle, and processing a much larger and more powerful organization.

FLIGHT TO THE JUNGLE

Sihanouk continued his anti-communist crusade, with his main blows falling on the Pracheachon, whose newspaper he closed and whose leaders he imprisoned. Pracheachon was effectively destroyed. Communist leaders went to ground. The Vietnamese had urged them to begin political struggle in Cambodia but this was suicidal. Tou Samouth, Pol Pot's old mentor, vanished in July 1962, and it was assumed that the police had caught him. Another possibility, given that no other members of the Cambodian Communist Party were arrested (the arrest and torture of one generally led to the arrests of others), is that Pol Pot himself was involved. Yet another story was that Sieu Heng had handed Tou Samouth over to the police, and two witnesses later corroborated this. Whatever the truth, the consequence was that Pol Pot became Acting General Secretary of the Party.

Soon afterwards, Pol Pot disappeared into the jungle. A student demonstration in Siem Reap had led to a police crackdown, and for the first time Lon Nol, Sihanouk's Defence Minister, included the names of Pol Pot (as Saloth Sar) and Ieng Sary on a list of thirty-four targets for arrest. Pol Pot was confirmed as Secretary-General of the Communist Party of Cambodia, and Ieng Sary was confirmed as a senior member of the Central Committee.

To avoid arrest, the two men decided to head for the eastern part of the country, near the Vietnamese border. Pol Pot was to spend the next seven years hiding from the police, apart from a brief period in North Vietnam and China. He was thus to be effectively isolated from world events, receiving all news via North Vietnamese and Chinese radio broadcasts. During much of this period he and his Cambodian colleagues were guarded by Vietnamese troops, unable to leave their camp without permission. Pol Pot gave himself over to educating the converted – his time was spent in endless discussions with communists, and in planning the future Cambodian state. Pol Pot went to China in 1966 just as the 'Cultural Revolution' was beginning, when Chinese intellectuals and 'class enemies' were subject to the attacks of the Red Guards – a sort of communist youth movement, which approached its task with indiscriminate iconoclasm, never too bothered with inconvenient facts and probably enjoying, as might many teenagers and young people, the officially approved chance to dominate its elders. A part of the Cultural Revolution hinged upon the idea that urban intellectuals should work in the fields, as this would give them a better understanding of a peasant revolution. This notion clearly impressed Pol Pot, with disastrous consequences later for the Cambodian élite.

During this period Pol Pot was based at Office 100, a mobile base which moved between Vietnam and Cambodia depending on military circumstances. Sihanouk, who was becoming increasingly anti-American as the war between North and South Vietnam hotted up, now allowed rights of passage to Vietnamese troops,

and also agreed that the Cambodian port of
Kompong Som could be used as an entry point
for arms from China, destined for the North
Vietnamese. This policy of co-operation with
the North Vietnamese was highly dangerous,
since it meant that Cambodia was no longer
truly neutral. Cambodians worried about
Sihanouk's policies, while Sihanouk responded by trying to suppress dissent, something which actually tended to drive more
Cambodians into the arms of the communists
and the resistance.

Things began to improve for Pol Pot when he
went to North Vietnam in 1965. There he
met many Cambodians who were being
trained by the North Vietnamese (though this
would lead to doubts later about where their
true loyalties lay), as well as his North
Vietnamese mentors. He was later to claim

that the part he played in the Cambodian revolution was robustly independent of the Vietnamese Party, but given that the North Vietnamese allowed him to go on to China in 1966, this is highly unlikely. The Vietnamese wanted the Cambodian Communist Party to co-operate with Sihanouk, because of the help he gave to them, but this idea was clearly an anathema to Pol Pot. The Chinese were apparently less domineering and Pol Pot must have been greatly impressed by the scale of success of the Chinese revolution and the enormous forces it marshalled – for example, the new edition of *The Quotations of Chairman Mao*, the famous 'Little Red Book', had a print run of 200 million copies.

In 1966 elections were again held for the National Assembly in Cambodia, and this time Sihanouk did not interfere with the process. The balance of the National Assembly was right-wing, though a few communists were elected, and the Assembly named Lon Nol Prime Minister, an ominous development for the communists.

The Cambodian communists now moved their headquarters to Ratanakiri, deep in the hinterland, to avoid the increasingly frequent raids by US bombers and US and South Vietnamese ground forces on the border where Office 100 had operated. The area around Ratanakiri was still inhabited by tribespeople who spoke their own languages and practised primitive agriculture. They didn't use money, and other aspects of tribal society there also appealed to communists – there was no social inequality and, of course, the tribespeople had no political ideology, which made them ideal converts. Like the

Communist Party they hated the Phnom Penh regime, and the commercialism which was making inroads into their territory so as to develop its resources.

Rebellion broke out in 1967 at Samlaut in Battambang Province. Peasants had been selling rice directly to the Vietnamese, without paying tax. Lon Nol sent soldiers into the countryside to enforce tax payment; two were killed, and Lon Nol reacted savagely, sending large reinforcements. Peasants were beaten up and interrogated, and in one battle the militia killed over 1000 communists, collecting their heads to verify the count. In Phnom Penh Sihanouk rounded on left-wingers whom he suspected of co-ordinating the insurrection, and the remaining communists, including those in the National Assembly, had to flee. Sihanouk's repression continued after the peasant uprising had been put down; he suspected the Vietnamese of having had a hand in it, and furthermore, copies of Mao's 'Little Red Book' had begun to circulate in French and Chinese editions. To pre-empt radical activity against the Government, Sihanouk ordered his police to execute suspects. This led to an exodus of radicals, including the last radical member of the National Assembly, and of many students and teachers. These events deeply worried the communists, who felt that they could not really come out in the open against Sihanouk because his forces of repression were simply too powerful. It was at this time, September 1967, that Pol Pot made the arduous two-week trip on foot from Office 100, where he had lingered for a few months, to Ratanakiri. He caught malaria *en route*.

The position of the Cambodian Communist

Party was now dire. It had lost its urban base, it had no weapons for an armed struggle, and politically it was weak. Sihanouk's forces in 1968 began to seek out communist forces more actively, and there were many skirmishes, though generally involving tens rather than hundreds of resistance fighters. Nonetheless, these small groups were considered the foundation stones of the Revolutionary Army. Sihanouk was also courting the Americans, partly perhaps because of the failure of the Tet Offensive in South Vietnam in January and February 1968, in which the Vietnamese communist guerrilla forces, the Vietcong, were decimated after much hard fighting, and the Americans responded by requesting the right to cross the Cambodian border to root out fugitive Vietnamese forces. This posed a further threat to Pol Pot, and he spent much of the time simply trying to avoid capture from the forces arrayed against him.

Sihanouk renewed full diplomatic relations with America in 1969, hoping for greater US aid to prop up his regime. But the Americans were much more interested in bombing North Vietnamese bases in Cambodia. This bombing, even by the standards of the time, was not accurate – US maps of enemy bases were inaccurate, and unknown numbers of Cambodian civilians perished. The effect was to drive many people, in border areas especially, to join the communists; the bombing also drove the Vietnamese away from the border areas, further into Cambodia. It is not clear whether Sihanouk authorized the American bombing, but many Cambodians thought so, so that the net result of his rapprochement with the USA was greater insecurity for his regime. The situation became slightly surreal. Both Sihanouk and the North Vietnamese pretended that there were no Vietnamese in Cambodia, yet the Americans were bombing them without the knowledge of their own population; meanwhile Sihanouk and the North Vietnamese were allies, while Cambodian government forces fought Khmer Rouge units which were frequently Vietnamese led!

Lon Nol now took over government, the National Assembly having voted Sihanouk out of the office of Chief of State during his annual holiday in France on 19 March 1970. Lon Nol had already increased his assaults on communist forces, and had ordered Vietnamese forces – albeit with no effect – out of the country. From Pol Pot's point of view this was a wonderful development. Because of the coup, Sihanouk was now in exile in China and the Vietnamese continued to urge cooperation with him, at least in the sense of using him as a figurehead for a 'National Front', so as to garner the support he still commanded in some rural areas. This Pol Pot could do, as Sihanouk was no longer a threat; he could then dump Sihanouk once power had been attained. Additionally, Pol Pot now had a military alliance with the North Vietnamese, Lon Nol having now effectively declared war on them. And there was no doubt that the the battle-hardened Vietnamese would be able to deal easily with the Cambodian Army. A further bonus, at least in the military sense, was that hundreds of Cambodians trained in North Vietnam returned to join the fray.

ARMED STRUGGLE
AND VICTORY

The Vietnamese were highly energetic, training the Cambodians for guerrilla warfare, and virtually press-ganging large numbers of them to fight for Sihanouk and his National Front. Numbers were further increased by many people who had fled after the coup, when pro-Sihanouk demonstrations had been brutally put down. The South Vietnamese and the Americans responded in the spring of 1970 by invading Cambodia in support of

War in Cambodia, 1970

Lon Nol's forces. Many young Cambodians also volunteered to fight for Lon Nol's forces in order to drive out the Vietnamese; in October 1970 Lon Nol had declared Cambodia a republic – the Khmer Republic – something which appealed to nationalist sentiments. But his new recruits, poorly trained, suffered many casualties fighting the Vietnamese. The Cambodian communists were able significantly to build up their organization, given Vietnamese dominance in the civil war; a large Party meeting was held in July 1971 at which the Central Committee was enlarged and to which larger numbers of cadres (sixty-one) were invited, reflecting the success of the Party in attracting recruits. At about the same time, Lon Nol had regrouped his forces and launched a major offensive; this had crumbled by December in the face of Vietnamese military superiority and his forces

47

were thrown back on the defensive, giving the Khmer Rouge a free hand to develop its policies, and expand recruitment and training. Sinisterly, though, and despite Party injunctions to convert the populace gently, Khmer Rouge units were dictatorial, and, as the civil war continued, began to treat the civilian population much as Lon Nol's troops did. Lon Nol's area of authority was rapidly shrinking as large tracts of the country were abandoned by his forces, ending up centred on a refugee-swollen Phnom Penh. His American sponsors were preoccupied with withdrawal from South Vietnam – something which formed part of US President Richard Nixon's election platform – and of course, the anti-war movement was growing increasingly strong in the USA.

At the end of 1973 the North Vietnamese

agreed a cease-fire with the Americans, part of whose terms were that the Vietnamese withdraw from Cambodia. This was a blow to Pol Pot as it left him exposed to Lon Nol's forces; as Secretary-General of the Khmer Communist Party, he was also leader of the Khmer Rouge guerrillas. The Party organization was inadequately trained and developed to administer the areas of the country it controlled, and militarily it was not nearly so well-organized and proficient as the Vietnamese. Indeed, in the rush to train cadres, Marxist-Leninist principles, such as the innate superiority of the proletariat, were effectively taught by rote, with no room for discussion or disagreement. This simple-minded spreading of communist doctrine would lead to a monolithic and inflexible Party, where to question any principle, whatever its applicability, was to reveal revisionism, which in many cases was enough to bring the death penalty for the unfortunate questioner.

During the Vietnamese withdrawal, those Cambodians who had trained in Vietnam came to be suspected of divided loyalties, and many were demoted or executed. Large numbers chose to leave with the Vietnamese. Khmer Rouge units actually fought against Vietnamese units in attempts to seize their heavy weapons. In communist-controlled areas, collective farms were established, people were forced to wear black peasant uniform, Buddhism was suppressed, and young people were removed and inducted into communist youth groups. To add to the catalogue of horrors for the Cambodian people, the US resumed its bombing campaign, since one of the terms of the cease-fire meant that it could no longer bomb Laos or Vietnam. The scale of the bombing was massive – 250,000 tons were dropped – and must have driven many peasants into the arms of the communists or caused them to flee to the cities, which were safe havens as the Americans were not bombing Government-controlled areas. The communists declared these refugees *personae non gratae*, on the grounds that they had effectively abandoned their 'superior' peasant heritage. The bombing campaign did, however, delay a communist takeover for two years.

The communists' attack in 1973 was broken by the American bombing. They tried again in 1974 – by which time US forces had finally quit Vietnam for good – and, despite increasingly desperate resistance, succeeded in cutting off the Government forces' supply

routes, apart from air transport and the
Mekong River. The final communist assault
began on 1 January 1975. In early April Lon
Nol fled, and the US Ambassador and other
foreigners were airlifted out. On 17 April
communist forces entered Phnom Penh.
They had been indoctrinated to regard the
citizens and refugees as enemies, and within
twenty-four hours had ordered the city to be
evacuated, which was accomplished in a
week. Where all the evacuees were supposed
to go, what they were supposed to eat, were
questions that were ignored, and in the mass
exodus many thousands – including Pol Pot's
elder brother Saloth Chhay – starved to death
or died of disease as they wandered aimlessly
over the country. This process was repeated
in the other cities that the communists
captured – in total 2 million Cambodians
were forced out of the cities. Money, private

French refugees from Phnom Penh arrive in Paris, May 1975

enterprise and private property were abolished.

Soon after Pol Pot's success, the Chinese offered technical assistance and massive economic aid to help rebuild the country. Sihanouk returned to the country after Chinese pressure on the Khmer Rouge and was briefly a figurehead Chief of State of the Khmer Republic, 1975–6. The Vietnamese, (the North had conquered the South by 1975, and in 1976 the country was reunified as the Socialist Republic of Vietnam), sent a new ambassador to Phnom Penh and were in general conciliatory, as clashes had broken out over islands in the Gulf of Thailand, where Cambodia sought access to offshore oil.

The communists' main task was to form a government and this they did behind the façade of the Revolutionary Organization, which was part of the National Front and in theory still regarded Sihanouk as head of state. All the senior communists, including Pol Pot (Saloth Sar) were using revolutionary names; the culture of secrecy and non-admission of actual responsibility, a hangover from the Party's days of persecution, continued. Ministries were divided out between eleven of Pol Pot's close associates, and two of their wives. Five were to be purged before the fall of his regime.

Pol Pot's name first appeared publicly in April 1976 during the election campaign for the People's Representative Assembly, which met to approve the Government of Democratic Kampuchea (DK), with Pol Pot as Prime Minister, and then dissolved itself. Also in April, Sihanouk resigned after the death of the

Khmer Rouge soldiers in Phnom Penh, May 1975

Chinese Prime Minister, Zhou Enlai, his most consistent supporter. He recognized that he had no real role in a communist government, and he was put under house arrest in the royal palace until 1978. He was not killed, however, as he was deemed to have participated in the revolution.

The problem of Vietnamese dominance occupied the new regime, as much resentment was felt at the way Vietnam had controlled the Cambodians during the revolution. Pol Pot and his government subscribed to the notion that non-communist South-East Asia – Burma (now Myanmar), Malaysia and Thailand – were themselves being rapidly communized and would aid Cambodian ambitions to contain Vietnam. This showed how isolated they were from true political developments. Not one of these countries would become communist (although Burma had become a socialist republic in 1974), despite much talk in the USA and elsewhere of the 'domino theory'.

In August 1976 Pol Pot revealed his Four-Year Plan, which set out the collectivization of agriculture, the nationalization of industry, and the financing of the modernization of all aspects of the economy through increased agricultural exports. The plan was drawn up in a vacuum with no reference to actual conditions in the country after the civil war, or even to general conditions in what everyone had now to call Kampuchea. The visions of smokestack industries, so dear to the communist traditionalist, were just that, visions. Cambodia lacks most of the resources necessary for heavy industry, including coal and steel. It would also need to go through a

Massive labour force at a construction site, 1977

stage of establishing light industries in order to pay for heavy industry, and the Government had no real idea even of what light industry it required.

Those in charge of implementing the Four-Year Plan caused untold misery in their attempts to meet its targets. Part of the plan was to triple the output of rice, with the necessary physical labour of preparing the countryside for paddy fields – irrigation, dykes and villages had to be built in virgin forest – being supplied by the evacuees from Phnom Penh of 17 April 1975. In horrible conditions, many thousands died. Production was much lower than had been planned, but because of the demand for exports, in part to fund an increased defence programme, the officials carrying out the plan designated the crops needed to feed the population as surplus. The consequent effects were calamitous for the population, fewer and fewer of whom were able to work because of malnutrition. Their condition was made worse by the regime's insistence on traditional Cambodian medicine. False reports of success flowed up the organization.

The Four-Year Plan also included the repression of Cambodian culture, to be replaced by revolutionary songs and approved reading. Schools, it was said, would be opened – although apparently, apart from some primary schools, they were not. Education was considered unimportant to revolutionary workers in Kampuchea, taking second place to work.

Pol Pot also opened the Tuol Sleng interrogation centre, otherwise known as S-21. In the years he was in power, over 20,000 men, women and children passed through the centre, and virtually none came out alive. Much of Pol Pot's life is described in the 'confessions' that were routinely extracted from prisoners in Tuol Sleng. The centre was the visible symbol of the regime's paranoia, so much so that at one stage it even turned on itself and executed sixty of its own employees. Confessions would detail links between the CIA, the Soviet Union, the Vietnamese; in other words, many would not bear the most superficial rational scrutiny. Even Pol Pot's oldest friends were not immune from purging, and their confessions testify to their utter surprise at their situation. Once in Tuol Sleng, though, declarations of innocence were regarded as being as treasonable as admissions of guilt.

Inside Tuel Sleng interrogation centre

Confessions led to more arrests, more confessions, and increased paranoia within the leadership of the Party.

COLLAPSE OF THE REGIME

Meanwhile skirmishes with Vietnam continued through into 1976, with both countries mounting border raids. These died down because the Kampucheans did not feel they had the military muscle to attempt anything more ambitious. After Mao Tse-tung's death that year, a promise of increased military aid for Kampuchea was given by China, whose own relations with Vietnam were deteriorating (the Chinese actually

Anti-Khmer Rouge fighters near the Thai border, 1979

briefly invaded Vietnam in 1979). The Khmer Rouge moved troops across the country and began to attack civilians in Vietnam, both by shelling and by making hit-and-run raids, in early 1977. (While this was going on, the Kampucheans were also hunting down ethnic Vietnamese in their own country and killing them.) The Vietnamese proposed a cease-fire in June 1977 but the Kampucheans were uninterested – Pol Pot was growing increasingly worried about Vietnamese subversion. Shelling of Vietnamese territory was stepped up in August and September, and Vietnamese civilians were massacred and their livestock seized. Under pressure from the Chinese, Pol Pot finally declared the existence of the Communist Party of Kampuchea on 27 September 1977. That speech was recorded, however, for Pol Pot left before the broadcast for Beijing and North Korea to confer with his sponsors. In his absence, the Vietnamese struck back against the border incursions. They then mustered larger forces and made a heavy attack on December 1977 which made real inroads into Kampuchea. This was intended as a deterrent to continuing Kampuchean raids. Instead, Pol Pot's government broke off relations with Hanoi. The Vietnamese withdrew taking many prisoners, and also civilians who were disenchanted with life under the Khmer Rouge. Vietnam probably expected a cease-fire but this was not forthcoming; instead, there were more Kampuchean raids, with the Chinese continuing to aid the Khmer Rouge. The Vietnamese began to think in terms of political warfare – effectively, of replacing the Pol Pot regime. The response was an opening up of the country as a counter to Vietnamese propaganda statements. Pol Pot relaxed some of his dress restrictions, opened more schools, and invited foreign delegations to witness the success of the Kampuchean revolution. An amnesty was even granted to those accused of working for the Vietnamese or the CIA! None of this, however, helped the military in the eastern part of Cambodia who had allowed the Vietnamese in – despite having been congratulated after the Vietnamese withdrawal, they were now purged, with perhaps 100,000 people being executed.

The Vietnamese renewed their attack on Kampuchea on 24 December 1978, this time with a full-scale army of fourteen divisions. By 2 January 1979 some commando units had actually reached Phnom Penh, where they attempted to capture Sihanouk. But Pol Pot had him spirited to the north of the country

Refugees fleeing to Thailand, 1979

until 5 January. On the 6th, he suggested that Sihanouk should represent him in Beijing to request more aid of the Chinese. Sihanouk was doubtless extremely happy to accept and thus leave the country. The commandos were followed on 7 January by the main body of the Vietnamese Army. The Kampuchean Government fled by train, while Pol Pot was whisked away by helicopter to Thailand.

The forces of Democratic Kampuchea fled to the north-west, mainly to Thailand, and the communist cadres sought to join them. Kampuchean peasants rose in large numbers against their erstwhile oppressors, killing or expelling them. Forlorn refugees took to the roads to return to their homes and find their relatives. The rice crop was left to rot in the fields. Camps were set up in Thailand for DK refugees and they began to reorganize the

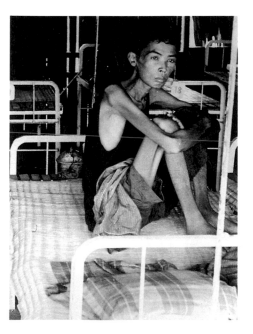

Starvation in Cambodia, 1979

struggle against the new Vietnamese puppet government of Kampuchea. The Khmer Rouge were recognized as a government-in-exile by China and the USA (still smarting from its defeat by the Vietnamese), and given a seat at the UN, though this was later disguised as being a National Front seat.

After this Pol Pot disappeared from public view, last granting an interview to a journalist in December 1979. But his troops still regularly infiltrated Kampuchea, fighting the Vietnamese and leaving mines scattered randomly throughout the country, causing many thousands of injuries, which were still continuing through into the 1990s. The Vietnamese-supported government remained in power after Vietnam's withdrawal in 1988 (completed in 1989), though in 1991 an agreement was signed in Paris for an interim to have affected him particularly, nor does the fact that he has effectively ensured over 1 million deaths: his view of the revolution was that, on balance, it was carried out correctly, and that he has no reason to change his spots. Pol Pot's is a tale of complete moral blindness, where half-digested notions were followed unquestioningly, where petty fears and paranoias were translated into terror for others, others who were treated with absolute indifference, not as human beings.

FURTHER MINI SERIES
INCLUDE

THEY DIED TOO YOUNG

Elvis
James Dean
Buddy Holly
Jimi Hendrix
Sid Vicious
Marc Bolan
Ayrton Senna
Marilyn Monroe
Jim Morrison

Prince Sihanouk in the 1970s

government under UN supervision. Eventually, in May 1995, elections were held under UN supervision, and a rather ramshackle coalition government came into power, with the participation of Sihanouk. In September of that year a new constitution re-established the monarchy. The Coalition Government was then jointly led by Sihanouk's son, Ranariddh, and Hun Sen. In all these changes the DK representatives were consulted, and the Khmer Rouge agreed to some concessions. But there have been several well-publicized killings and kidnappings, including those of Westerners in the recent years, although it is hard to attribute responsibility, given the relatively lawless state of Cambodia. The Thais have stated that Pol Pot has returned to a new camp in Cambodia. Very few Cambodians would like to see him return to power.

On balance, what can one think of Pol Pot? He spent his early years in the rarefied atmosphere of the royal palace, cut off from ordinary Cambodian life. He then, more by luck than ability, it seems, managed to prolong his education further than most of his countrymen, both in Cambodia and France, always part of a tiny élite, even if never a true intellectual. After a few years in the relatively 'normal' role of teacher, he was again cut off in the jungle, surrounded by acolytes and those of a similar persuasion, where ideas could be proposed and discussed with no reference to reality or practicality. When he gained power he cut himself off from the people behind a veil of secrecy and paranoia. In power he tried to enforce his ideas in an utterly dogmatic manner. That the effects of his policies were catastrophic does not seem

Khmer Rouge leaders in western Cambodia, 1986
(Pol Pot on the right)

THEY DIED TOO YOUNG

Malcolm X
Kurt Cobain
River Phoenix
John Lennon
Glenn Miller
Isadora Duncan
Rudolph Valentino
Freddie Mercury
Bob Marley

FURTHER MINI SERIES
INCLUDE

HEROES OF THE WILD WEST

General Custer
Butch Cassidy and the Sundance Kid
Billy the Kid
Annie Oakley
Buffalo Bill
Geronimo
Wyatt Earp
Doc Holliday
Sitting Bull
Jesse James